PATTERNS EVERYWHERE

LISA VARCHOL PERRON

M Millbrook Press / Minneapolis

Step outside. Let's find designs—

branching, cracking, spirals, lines.

Search the earth, the seas, the air.

Patterns, patterns everywhere.

WHAT IS A PATTERN?

A pattern is a sequence that repeats in a predictable way. Nature is full of them! Some of nature's patterns are made of repeating geometric shapes. Other patterns are created by color or spacing.

Veins on leaves extend like shoots,
bringing water up from roots,
helping plants stay strong and green.
Patterns, patterns to be seen.

LEAF VEINS

A leaf's veins carry water and nutrients to and from the plant's roots. The pattern of leaf veins, called venation, varies depending on the type of plant. Most fruit trees have wide leaves with a netted pattern—smaller veins branching out from a central one. The long and narrow leaves of corn and grasses have a parallel pattern— veins running lengthwise along the leaf.

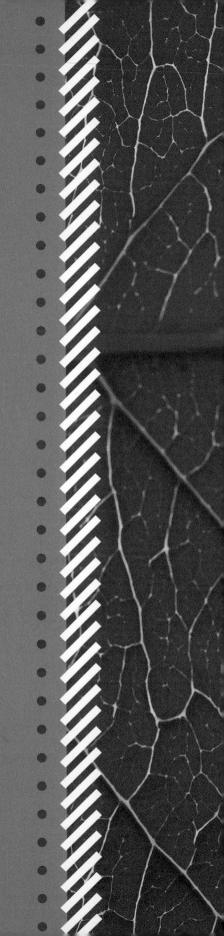

Ridges dip to valleys low—

spaced and even, row by row.

Waters etch and soils creep.

Patterns, patterns wide and deep.

RIDGES AND VALLEYS

Over time, ridges and valleys tend to become evenly spaced, like the teeth on a comb. Valleys are carved by rivers, which collect water from rain. The farther away a river is from neighboring rivers, the more water it can collect. If two rivers are far apart, a new one can form in between. But if a river is too close to its neighbor, it won't be able to collect enough rainwater and the valley it created will fill in with soil in a process called soil creep. That's why the spacing of valleys tends to be consistent—not too close and not too far apart.

Dunes arise from wind on land,

lifting, drifting grains of sand.

Crescent moon or desert star.

Patterns, patterns near and far.

SAND DUNES

Dunes come in different shapes and sizes, depending on the speed and direction of the wind that forms them, the amount of sand in the area, and the surrounding vegetation. One common type is a barchan dune, which resembles a crescent moon. Star dunes have a central pyramid with three or more arms. Other types include longitudinal, transverse, and parabolic dunes.

Rivers bend like twisting snakes,

winding toward vast seas or lakes.

Over time, the banks can change.

Patterns, patterns rearrange.

MEANDERING RIVERS

Many rivers that flow over gently sloping ground develop a snakelike, or meandering, pattern. As water travels around a bend, it flows faster near the outer edge, or bank, causing the ground to wear away, or erode, and the inner bank to build up bits of rock and soil called sediment. Over time, the combination of erosion and sediment buildup changes the path of a river.

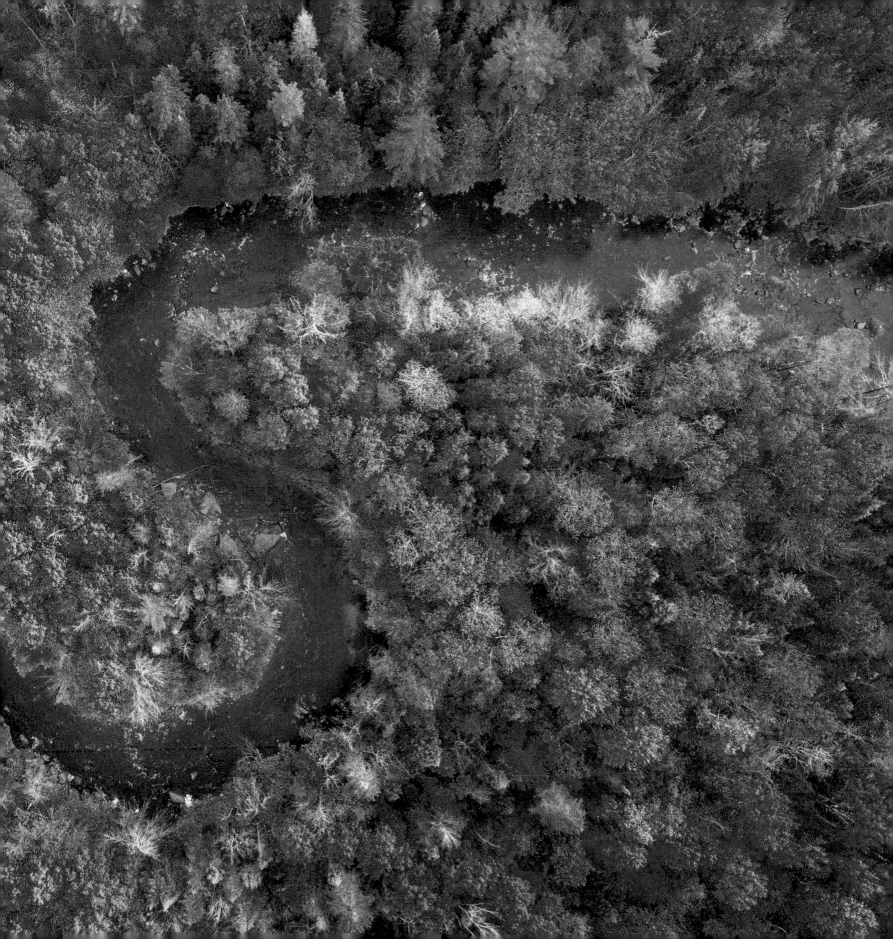

Coral creatures dot the seas,

shaped like mushrooms, brains, and trees.

Fueled by steady streams of light.

Patterns, patterns bold and bright.

CORALS

Corals are sea animals. Some of them build hard structures called reefs. There are about six thousand types of corals with a variety of patterns, including mushroom coral, brain coral, and staghorn coral—which resembles antlers or the branches of a tree. Their bright colors come from algae, plantlike organisms that use sunlight to make food for themselves and the corals they live on.

Ripples stretch across the beach,

marking where the waves can reach.

Sand responds to water's flow.

Patterns, patterns come and go.

WAVE RIPPLES

At high tide, the water level of the ocean rises and covers much of the shore. At low tide, the water level falls and exposes more beach. Waves cause water to circle around beneath the surface, pick up loose grains of sand, and set them back down again. When the tide goes out, the water leaves behind ripples formed by this process. Usually, these ripples will disappear and re-form with the next high tide. The size of the waves, the depth of the water, and the size of the sand grains determine how far apart the ripples are spaced.

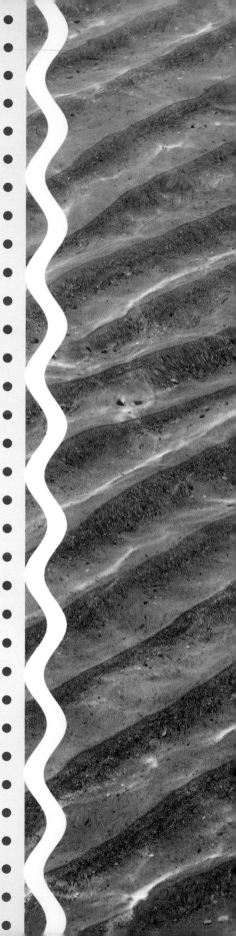

Buoyant bubbles meet and stick.

Foam emerges, rich and thick.

Churned and stiffened in a storm.

Patterns, patterns taking form.

SEA FOAM

Masses of bubbles stick together to create foam. Sea foam almost always forms near shorelines, where waves mix, or churn, the water. If you look closely at three bubbles stuck together, you will see that they bend to allow for the tightest fit. Sea foam is more than just water. It also includes dissolved substances from small plants and animals in the ocean.

Stripes of color paint the earth,

layered long before our birth.

Bands of red and black and gold.

Patterns, patterns to behold.

LAYERED EARTH

Visible layers, or strata, can appear in areas that have experienced a range of climates. In the Painted Hills of Oregon, each stripe contains a different type of soil from various points in time—up to thirty-five million years ago! The red layers contain large amounts of iron oxide from wet and warm periods. Drier, cooler eras created the yellow and gold stripes. Black layers contain a type of coal formed from decaying plants.

Lava splits in columned cracks.

Fluid cools and rock contracts.

Giant pillars here to stay.

Patterns, patterns on display.

BASALT COLUMNS

In a volcanic eruption, melted rock called magma rises through openings, or vents, in Earth's crust. Lava columns form when thick magma begins to cool and crack at the surface. Those cracks spread downward into the cooling volcanic rock, called basalt, creating pillars. Many of these pillars are six-sided, or hexagonal, like the walls of a honeycomb. Hexagon shapes are common in nature because they allow for tight fits with no wasted space.

Tiny treasures dot the sky.

Icy crystals, frozen high.

Branching snowflakes meet the ground.

Patterns, patterns all around.

SNOWFLAKES

Snowflakes are ice crystals that take on various shapes depending on the temperature and moisture in the air when they formed. Because of the way water molecules bind together, snowflakes have six sides. Branching snowflakes create smaller and smaller repeated patterns called fractals.

Air grows warmer. Wet mud dries.

Cracks appear. A spring surprise!

Soon a network is complete.

Patterns, patterns at our feet.

MUD CRACKS

When soil that was wet begins to dry, the surface cracks as the soil starts to shrink, or contract. Further drying leads the cracks to spread and connect, forming a network of repeated shapes without gaps or overlaps called a tessellation network. This is similar to the process that forms basalt columns but is caused by drying instead of cooling.

Spirals snuggle, safe and tight.

Growing when the time is right.

Center point and moving curve.

Patterns, patterns to observe.

SPIRAL PLANTS AND ANIMALS

Spiral shapes allow plants and animals to maintain strength and stability as they grow. Examples in nature include pine cones, flower petals, pineapples, artichokes, snail shells, and sheep horns. A mathematical form called a Fibonacci sequence describes a special kind of spiral shape that becomes wider as it grows.

Nature waits beyond the door.

Endless wonders to explore.

What might *you* discover there?

Patterns, patterns everywhere.

PATTERNS REALLY ARE EVERYWHERE!

- Patterns exist everywhere on Earth and on other planets too! What patterns have you observed in nature? Where have you seen them?

- The words in this book also follow a pattern. The first two lines of every stanza rhyme with each other, and then the next two lines rhyme. This is called an AABB rhyme pattern.

- Being able to identify and compare patterns helps us predict how those patterns will repeat. This is an important math skill!

ACTIVITY

Gather a sketchbook and pencil and go outside. Draw pictures of a pattern that you see. Is it similar to any other patterns in nature?

- If you see the inside of a sunflower, you might be reminded of mud cracks or sea foam bubbles packed closely together in a tessellation pattern.

- Maybe you'll find a fern and notice how it branches into smaller and smaller versions of itself, similar to a branching snowflake. This is a fractal pattern.

- In the garden, you might come across a pea plant with tendrils curling in a spiral shape that helps the plant stay strong as it grows, just like a snail's shell.

- Or consider making your own pattern by lining up items you find in nature. Leaf, rock, leaf, rock would be an alternating, or ABAB, pattern, which also occurs in alternating ridges and valleys.

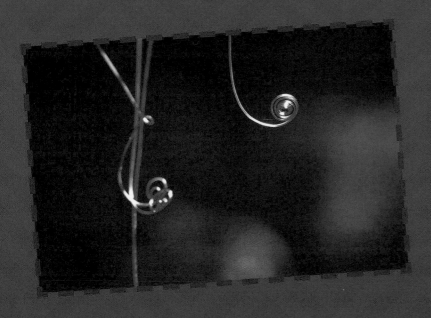

GLOSSARY

algae: organisms that use sunlight to make food, like plants, but without roots, stems, and leaves. They are usually found in water.

bank: the land on either side of a river

basalt: a dark, fine-grained volcanic rock formed when lava cools

buoyant: able to float

climate: the average weather conditions in a place over time

column: a pillar with two identical shapes on either end

crystal: a solid material with molecules that fit together in a repeating pattern

design: a decorative pattern

dune: a mound of sand formed by wind or water

Fibonacci sequence: a sequence of numbers where each number equals the sum of the two numbers before it. The sequence appears in nature in multiple ways such as the number of petals on a sunflower and the scales on a pine cone.

molecule: a very small particle of a specific substance

period: a portion of time

ridge: a long, narrow stretch of a hilltop or mountain

soil creep: the slow, downhill movement of rock and soil

valley: a low area of land between hills or mountains

vein: a tubelike structure within a leaf that carries water and nutrients to different parts of a plant and also helps a leaf hold its shape

FURTHER READING

Books

Campbell, Sarah C. *Growing Patterns: Fibonacci Numbers in Nature.* Honesdale, PA: Boyds Mills, 2010.
Learn more about growing patterns in nature.

Campbell, Sarah C. *Mysterious Patterns: Finding Fractals in Nature.* Honesdale, PA: Boyds Mills, 2014.
Dive deeper into branching patterns in nature.

Cleary, Brian P. *A-B-A-B-A—a Book of Pattern Play.* Minneapolis: Millbrook Press, 2014.
Practice predicting patterns of shapes, colors, objects, and numbers!

Goldstone, Bruce. *I See a Pattern Here.* New York: Henry Holt, 2015.
Explore assorted patterns in nature as well as human-made patterns, like mosaics.

Sidman, Joyce. *Swirl by Swirl: Spirals in Nature.* New York: HMH Books for Young Readers, 2011.
Find out more about the beauty and strength of spiral shapes in the natural world.

Websites

How Is Coral Made?
https://www.wonderopolis.org/wonder/How-is-Coral-Made
Read about coral formation and current threats to coral reefs.

Snowflake Science
https://thehomeschoolscientist.com/snowflake-science/
Deepen your understanding of how snowflakes form.

What Is Geomorphology?
https://www.wonderopolis.org/wonder/What-Is-Geomorphology
Learn about the scientists who study the formation of valleys, rivers, basalt columns, sand dunes, mud cracks, and other landforms!

To Mia and Ada—two extraordinary explorers!

Acknowledgments: Thanks to Dr. Jerry Mitrovica and Dr. Taylor Perron for sharing their scientific expertise.

Text copyright © 2023 by Lisa Varchol Perron

Millbrook Press™
An imprint of Lerner Publishing Group, Inc.
241 First Avenue North
Minneapolis, MN 55401 USA

For reading levels and more information, look up this title at www.lernerbooks.com.

Designed by Viet Chu.

Main body text set in Adrianna.
Typeface provided by Chank.

Image credits: irin-k/shutterstock.com, pp. 2–3; by Simon Gakhar/Getty Images, pp. 4–5; Pat Tr/shutterstock.com, pp. 6–7; Matauw/shutterstock.com, p. 8; Gallo Images/Alamy Stock Photo, p. 9; by Marc Guitard/Getty Images, pp. 10–11; Vojce/shutterstock.com, p. 11; Keat Eung/shutterstock.com, p. 13 (right); Reinhard Dirscherl/Getty Images, p. 13 (left); George Pachantouris/Getty Images, pp. 14–15; shayes17/Getty Images, pp. 16–17; Emily Marie Wilson/shutterstock.com, pp. 18–19; Donna Carpenter/shutterstock.com, pp. 20–21; JonnyWolf/shutterstock.com, pp. 22–23; Tuul & Bruno Morandi/Getty Images, pp. 24–25; Cindy Robinson/Getty Images, p. 26; Isabelle OHara/shutterstock, p. 27; Dean Fikar/Getty Images, pp. 28–29; Marcia Straub/Getty Images, p. 30 (right); Kevin Wells Photography/shutterstock.com, p. 30 (left).

Cover images: Sergio Amiti/Getty Images; Tim Votapka/500px/Getty Images; santanor/istock/Getty Images; Dash Shemtoob/Getty Images; wsfurlan/Getty Images; by Dornveek Markkstyrn/Getty Images.

Library of Congress Cataloging-in-Publication Data

Names: Perron, Lisa Varchol, author.
Title: Patterns everywhere / by Lisa Varchol Perron.
Description: Minneapolis, MN : Millbrook Press , [2023] | Includes bibliographical references. | Audience: Ages 5–9 | Audience: Grades 2-3 | Summary: "When you take the time to look, you'll find that nature is full of patterns. Lyrical, rhyming verse and stunning photographs introduce young readers to patterns throughout the natural world"— Provided by publisher.
Identifiers: LCCN 2022020274 (print) | LCCN 2022020275 (ebook) | ISBN 9781728460420 (library binding) | ISBN 9781728485829 (ebook)
Subjects: LCSH: Pattern perception—Juvenile literature. | Nature—Juvenile literature.
Classification: LCC BF294 .P47 2023 (print) | LCC BF294 (ebook) | DDC 152.14/23—dc23/eng/20220705

LC record available at https://lccn.loc.gov/2022020274
LC ebook record available at https://lccn.loc.gov/2022020275

Manufactured in the United States of America
1-51509-50381-8/18/2022